SAVE MONEY:
Thrift and Consignment Clothes Shopping

Sandi Lynn

authorHOUSE®

AuthorHouse™
1663 Liberty Drive
Bloomington, IN 47403
www.authorhouse.com
Phone: 1-800-839-8640

First published by AuthorHouse 1/5/2010

ISBN: 978-1-4389-4698-6 (sc)

Printed in the United States of America
Bloomington, Indiana

This book is printed on acid-free paper.

Dedication

To my devoted parents, Commander Calvin C. Reed, USN, retired, and his first mate of nearly 60 years, my loving mom, Eunice Reed. Thank you for all you modeled for me. Abundance via frugality enhances my life to its fullest.

Frugality is one of the most beautiful and joyful words in the English language, and yet one that we are culturally cut off from understanding and enjoying. The consumption society has made us feel that happiness lies in having things, and has failed to teach us the happiness of not having things.

Elise Boulding

Table of Contents

1. Priorities in Wardrobe Additions: Your list 1

2. Where to Shop   11

3. Preparing for the Adventure   17

4. Efficiency Scanning List   21

5. Wardrobe Maximization   34

6. Closet Organization   47

7. Conservation Equals Your Abundance   52

8. Other Nifty Thrifty Deals   62

9. Referrals for Conscious Consumption   66

10. Celebration   70

Preface

In this easily understood handbook, you will learn the rewards of 'thrifty' shopping for you, your wallet and the environment. Locations to experience this adventure abound: thrift stores, consignment stores, cash for resale shops, the ever abundant garage sales and E-Bay. Occasionally you might gain rare items at an estate sale listed in the local newspaper. These are all explained in Chapter 2.

Would you have picked up this book without valuing greater financial benefits, or enjoying beauty and functionality, or considering the idea of conservation of our environment? These clothes-shopping tips can be used at retail shops, too. To sharpen your shopping skill sets and save money to deposit where you get the most fulfillments—you have arrived at the starting page. This handbook empowers readers to live fuller financial lives.

Like it, value it—or not—people notice your appearance when first meeting you. Your smile, words and clothing announce you to others. If money is tight or you prefer to spend it in others areas—for example, sports or travel—then this type of shopping offers a viable option. I began thrift and consignment shopping when my life journey included the leanness of single parenting that brought financial challenges. Along with substantial savings, I treasured how fantastic my sons looked on a dime. I later stretched into the realm of purchasing for myself. I have enjoyed the fun of acquiring an Ann Taylor silk blouse for $2.70, a Jones New York tweed jacket for $10.00, a quality Old Navy cotton blouse for $3.00, and a Dana Buchman wool black sweater with white trim for $9.00. I have purchased barely worn near-new casual flats for $5.00. What fun and fulfillment!

Shopper-tainment!

This book is designed as a 'play' guide to take with you on your quests. You will find 'ease of reference' to hone your shopping skills as you proceed down the aisles. You will learn how to sort what works best for you—first inside your closet—then on the racks. You will learn to clarify what you need and desire based on values.

A preview of the definition of frugality encompasses: resourcefulness and the art of paying careful attention to choices. These will assist much in the financial arena. Your alert attention will signal when yet another black sweater purchase consideration causes more emotional discomfort—just finding a home for it—than the supposed satisfaction you anticipated when buying it. Wise, 'thought-filled' choices epitomize a happy resourceful wardrobe owner. She can be you!

Frugality and de-cluttering become closet partners. In Chapter 5, you will learn what it takes to feel accomplished at integrating items for your optimum appearance. Enjoy a measure of peace knowing that your choices fit well and delight you. Before prancing off to shop, survey what you own by jumping ahead to this chapter to create a shopping list. This clarifies what you can add to expand your wardrobe—without cramping the closet. While list-making, you will encounter at least a few items—right there on your hangers, no less—that look tacky and counter to the image you seek to project. Clarify what you want to affirm about your unique self.

After all, the substance of who we are internally will stand out better through such external image boosters as hairstyle, nail care, makeup or none, and wardrobe. Make no mistake; the world needs the best you it can experience. You are integral to the whole.

After clarifying what to purchase, clothes shopping will be an area where you need never be unconscious again. For that matter, with practice, you can decrease impulse spending in other arenas. You will become a "seriously aware shopper" (SAS). This clear awareness of your needs and how they will, or will not fulfill you, offers another gem—simplifying your life. Furthermore, how nice would it feel to you to transfer excessive time spent impulse buying—often with little satisfaction—to conscious spending?

Inside you will find skill training that addresses stay-at-home mom and weekend dressers, career dressers and retired women. Chapter 1 will revisit the idea of enjoying comfort without forfeiting stylishness. Rather than worn sweatshirts and sweatpants, consider a well-fitting matched ensemble or quality fitting jeans with a top or sweater a slight step above your norm. At thrifty prices, look and feel your best. Call it dressing up every day! The caveat to this is a baby drooling regularly on an Anne Klein blouse. Fully savor your precious baby and forego that blouse, except for when the sitter arrives.

I describe some transformational skill-sets for shopping that contribute toward a long overdue return to sage stewardship. Since a good steward manages property entrusted to him/her, how would you spend this extra money you will see when you have read this book?

Besides the benefit you reap, our fragile globe also will, when you shop consciously and circulate (recycle) what is here, rather than relegate it to a trash dump. See www.storyofstuff.com, a resource mentioned in Chapter 9. By reusing existing items, you decrease the demand, and therefore production. Circulating clothes back into the economy provides savings to the next buyers and wages to workers. In interrelated communities, we all gain when we share.

Big bonus! The skills used in this book have saved me thousands of dollars over the decades, which I used for other important priorities. I have often averaged $55/month for clothing, which includes department store and boutique clearance racks. You need not spend so slight an amount unless it fulfills you. Since I enjoy what I wear, my desires are satisfied.

You too may save a bundle and wear top quality clothes with great satisfaction!

Sandi Lynn
Golden, Colorado

Chapter 1—Priorities in Wardrobe Additions: Your list

"I have three precious things which I hold fast and prize. The first is gentleness; the second is frugality; the third is humility, which keeps me from putting myself before others. Be gentle and you can be bold; be frugal and you can be liberal; avoid putting yourself before others and you can become a leader among men."

Lao Tzu

Okay, you are ready for a shopping trip. You need clothing or you desire a newer look. You want a spending fix! Whatever your motives—planning ahead will be worth the time spent.

First consider shopping from a purely functional perspective: what your daily life requires and what clothing will satisfy these activities. You may find that you're in the habit of purchasing several exercise pieces, when 'gym rat' is not a name your friends use to describe you. Do you see how adding purchases in the exercise category makes little sense? Shorts and jeans might be all you need. Regarding jeans, how many will suffice?

Quick! What answer comes to you? This will be revealing. Remember each additional item crowds your shelves, drawers or closet rod. You make it difficult to see what you own and/or crowd out what will augment your wardrobe.

Discouraging purchases that you desire as one of life's pleasures is not my goal. That approach will be explored further in the chapter. I assert, though, that you will find rewards if you train yourself to become a 'seriously aware shopper' (SAS). Americans consume far more than is sensible as shown in Chapter 7. To determine what works for you, first consider what your lifestyle entails. Career women need career clothing. They rarely need six pair of jeans. I own two nice jeans plus one for camping or occasional messy household work. Consider keeping no more than the right number. This approach offers freedom, not a mandate. When you reach the book's closet organization chapter, you will have the chance to ask yourself regarding each item if it decreases clutter by its versatility, or adds to clutter.

If you are a busy mom or a full time student, or both, what type and number of casual wardrobe pieces would you ideally focus most dollars toward? As to type—consider nice jeans, quality cotton—such as chino or cotton and spandex. Also, consider corduroys, different colored denims, even skirts rather than jeans! You may prefer skirts and sandals in the summer, rather than shorts—to feel more feminine and comfortable.

Another way to assess the quantity of clothes you need is to ask, "In one month how many outfits will I need?" If predominant time is spent in a dress-up career, how many suits, slacks, sweaters, and evening gowns do you need? If you are capable of wading through reams of clothing without stalling in daily decision-making time, then plenty of items work for you. For others, the abundant feeling lies in the thorough enjoyment of several cherished items and a speedy dressing process. Either way, no choice is right or wrong— just efficient for you. To relish abundance, see Chapter 7.

Purchase for the roles you live. As far as how many items to buy—personal values dictate our decisions.

The second shopping focus you might choose is to ask yourself: "What do I most prefer and why? Should I streamline the number of items to make decisions easier for me or accumulate many items for the fun of variety and excitement of the hunt?"

There is no right or wrong answer but it's a good idea to contemplate this question before progressing through this book. The goal is to focus your shopping to align with your values. No matter what your answer to the above question, you want to make pieces work well together on a daily and monthly basis to maximize your creative looks—with whatever you own.

From an affinity for red or black shoes to the food choices we make, everyone bases their decisions on values unique to them! The importance of consistency in what we declare we value and how we live those values takes center stage. To prove this for yourself, think of actions you have taken in the past that do not fit you. Have you ever said "yes" when you knew you meant "no"?

The reasons behind that in-congruency, and the path away from it, are many. They may be the subject of another manuscript. However, for this book, when did you last fool yourself about what you chose to give attention? How about TV watching, rather than soul-touching music and a bath that may have satisfied so much more? Have you colluded with a friend's untrue story, which made her feel better in the short term, but allowed you to avoid confronting her lack of authenticity?

These situations may represent disconnections with your values, which will be felt in your body as signals to get back on track. Become aware of your values, live within them and celebrate the benefits you reap in both wise cash outlays and peace of mind from living true to yourself.

Whether deciding based on what you require or what you prefer, a few moments preparing a list of what you need, will streamline the shopping process for you. This will require pre-scanning your apparel for what will complete it; e.g. do your slacks look faded and hang poorly? Is the lining worn out? Are you lacking the right color jacket to match a skirt? Does your wardrobe lack colors, consisting of mainly neutrals?

If current styles appeal to you, scan the July/ August Glamour magazine for fall and winter looks or the February/March issue for spring and summer. You can also check online for coming colors and styles to shop frugally and still align with the latest fashions.

If you have not already done so, please use the wardrobe organization ideas in Chapter 6 at which time you will create a shopping list.   Do you own clothing lines that flatter you and fit exceptionally well? For example: Ann Taylor, Banana Republic, Gap, Old Navy, J Crew, Express, St John's for knits, Casual Corner. They fit better due to the cuts the production team chooses for their patterns.

Knowing these designers or manufacturers prompts you to keep on the lookout for these labels when making selections to try on clothes. You can inspect these selected items later. You need to pull it from the rack on the first pass. You will regret if another customer captured what you returned to retrieve—and it was gone.

Construct a shopping 'adventure' list categorized by: jackets, jeans, dresses, suits, skirts, slacks/shorts, sweaters, tops like T-shirts, blouses, coats, accessories like scarves, belts, jewelry. Include shoes on the list –if you are up to the challenge of locating those never or barely worn. I have found unused packaged hosiery for a fraction of the department store cost so if you need hose, note that in accessories. Note preferred colors on your list.

Speaking of color, it is a very important variable, unless you expect to chop wood or milk cows in this outfit. Know your best colors and insist on purchases in those shades. The advantages abound: you will almost always reach for those items which make you look most attractive. You will have a better chance of matching what already resides in your closet. Your best colors are those that garner admiring compliments. If possible, carry a color palette. It is similar to an artist's palette for mixing several colors in one location. You can make your palette on a somewhat thick cardboard that is no larger than 5" x 8". Cut 1 to 1 1/2" x 2" fabric pieces with pinking shears, to prevent raveling. Glue them onto the cardboard. Seamstresses have these shears to prevent unraveling seams and they have fabric remnants to cut from, for a minimal price. Or maybe you know someone who might cut some swatches for you for a nominal fee. With time, you will memorize your colors and not need this tool.

Color caveats include:

A.   If you look washed out, or sickly in a warm cream color next to your face, you might wear it over black or navy or burgundy to feature the more ideal color by your face; e. g. layer with the beauty of a luscious cream sweater or jacket.

B.   If deep or vibrant colors do not enhance your natural coloring, but instead, announce their arrival before you do—stay with light colors by your face. Light colors can also be layered upon each other.

C.   If you like a color that is not normally your best, and it will be worn away from your face such as slacks, shorts, or a skirt, you could purchase it if you have a match for it in your best color next to your face; e.g. from my closet—orange shorts and a black or white top features the sunny orange far from my face. Other 'warm' colors with a yellow tone to them that I might wear in a skirt or shorts or capris are: yellow, gold, cream, rust, lime green, turquoise, coral and orange-red. In contrast, if you are of skin coloring that looks great in these colors, the ones you will tend to wear away from your face include: clear white, grey, forest green, clear red, burgundy or cranberry reds, bright and baby blue, light and bright pinks, deep and lavender purples, and dark blue green.

D.   For warm weather dressing, you also could wear a less than ideal color in a top if it allows much of the upper chest to show; e.g. in a tank top, with thin straps. The less attractive color may not detract much since it is somewhat away from the face. If a necklace contains your better colors, this might balance to enhance skin tones.

Overall, it is more efficient for shopping and matching purposes to stay within your best colors.

Back to your shopping list, you can add to your roll any items your friends may need if you know their taste—and you feel sure they will welcome thrift items. If they are not pleased with your purchase, you can often return it for credit within seven days, or gift it to any local church which has a clothing bank.

You can also add any non-clothing items elsewhere on the list if you are amenable to that kind of search. See Chapter 2 for particulars.

Your list will become a working tool to carry with you at all times as you await the arrival of your perfect purchase—assuming waiting works for you. After a long wait, I found a black leather Valerie Steven's skirt. Though the brand name became obsolete, the quality of its leather remained superb and the versatility broad. I wear it often.

Chapter 2—Where to Shop

"In the old days a man who saved money was a miser; nowadays he's a wonder."

Author Unknown

Whether 'scaling down' or not, experience and referrals will help locate the best local options for cost and value—to gain the highest quality while limiting the number of items. You want to 'like' garments enough to reach for them often.

Consignment stores accept recently purchased, 'gently used' articles. Those stores most resemble a retail shop or boutique in orderliness and ambiance. Clothes accepted for consignment by the store owner must be in good condition, cleaned and on hangers. Jewelry, hats, scarves and gloves are featured to demonstrate fashion ideas.

Clothes are marked down to a third or fourth of their original price tag. The owners are available to advise you on how something fits you or how the color accentuates your coloring. Since they speak from their own perspective, this can be an advantage in gaining a new viewpoint to stretch you outside your norm, or a disadvantage if you don't trust an owner's opinion. You will need to discern if they will be honest versus pushing the sale. You may sense both attitudes from owners. Ask them when their summer and winter sales tend to be offered and ask to be on their email or mailing list for notification. The first day of these sales provides the most selection.

Consignment stores contract with you to market your more valuable possessions in trade for a 40-60 percent allowance for their effort. You receive the other 40-60 percent after a two to four month showing. If they are not sold, you choose either to retrieve them or donate them. This decision is noted within the contract you sign.

On the other hand, thrift store shopping offers advantages that include the lowest prices next to garage sales. Thrift stores are in business to make money that will support their missions, such as training the disadvantaged or earning money to give to whatever mission they chose. These stores recycle what people have donated in clothing, small and large household items, major appliances, books, furniture, kitchen ware. They include framed pictures, lamps, rugs, unusual dishes and mugs, used medical equipment and toys. Make sure that purchases in these categories are both sturdy and can be repaired or cleaned, if needed. You can also find computer parts and tools.

When donating to thrift stores, you have the option of deducting a certain percentage of the donation on your taxes if you request the donation slip for tax documentation. Clothing represents about 50 percent of the merchandise in these stores and is available for four to five weeks. There are often brand new garments available. To recycle your used clothing, ask which thrift stores will pick up your items, thus saving you the trouble of hauling them yourself. During our current faltering economy, thrift store shopping provides relief from voracious consumerism.

Some thrift stores are orderly while some are crowded and less appealing. You will have few store staff to advise of if the color works for you.

If you can endure frequent chaos, you may enjoy special 'finds' due to the reluctance many have to frequent them—leaving you more possibilities. Unlike consignment stores, these clothes may not be cleaned before donation, so they will need cleaning, even though some items will come with dry-cleaning tags. When donated to the store, they are mixed in bins with any number of dirty items.

Call thrift stores beforehand to learn how and when sales are offered, and to verify store hours. Also ask if they are the newest store of that chain as these are nicer and often have better selections. Most accept credit cards and checks but you should inquire. Though not always true, stores located near higher priced homes might bring in extra goodies. Check addresses to map your journey if more than one store is visited. Many have seniors' days with discounts of 25-50 percent. Many thrift stores, such as Salvation Army, Savers, Goodwill, ARC (Association of Retarded Persons) and DAV (Disabled American Veterans) provide discounts on different colored tags on various days of the week, usually 50 percent. Brand name items are often not discounted at all. Since the quality is noteworthy, the slightly higher cost might be worth it to you. Christmas time and before school starts make good shopping days. The week before Halloween can be hectic.

Cash-for-resale shops offer to buy your item to sell at the price they wish. These stores pay less than could be returned at a consignment store. They do provide ready cash.

Garage sales seem a less attractive option for adult clothing due to time constraints in driving to different areas plus there is often no place to try on the items. However, prices can be superb. Garments may not be organized and selections may be scant. Garage sales work great for children's clothing since you can buy sizes ahead for what you expect in several years. They also are worth a visit when several homes in the neighborhood choose a weekend and they all feature their odds and ends. The last hours of the final day offer nice prices and better ability to negotiate than the first days. Take your kids to teach them how to negotiate and accept 'no' for an answer, when you are not willing to pay the stated price.

Estate sales are wonderful for antiques, laces and furs that can be remade if the fur retains its quality. Generally the entire estate house will be cleared so you can eventually obtain shelving and other unusual items, once the sale is over. Look on Google for your national location; e.g.

"estate sale + Denver" to find those who manage these sales and they will send you email notices of upcoming events.

E-bay buying will require knowing and requesting from the seller various measurements to make sure the garment will fit. You cannot try it on until you prepay and it arrives. Slacks require inseam measurements, and largest hip and waist measurements. Tops require sleeve length measurement. Purchases on E-bay can be exceptional as far as uniqueness and quality.

Chapter 3—Preparing for the Adventure

"Too many people spend money they haven't earned, to buy things they don't want, to impress people they don't like."

Will Rogers

Enjoy these shopping tips! On shopping day wear clothes and shoes that remove quickly for trying on garments. If sensible, wear anything you wish to match into the store since it is easier than carrying it. Avoid jewelry that may become entangled, such as large or drop earrings, long necklaces and scarves. For weekend shopping, a full skirt will allow you to try apparel under the skirt—should dressing rooms be full. If you plan to buy dress clothes, bring heels. You will find it painful to wear them for a shopping trip due to the time spent on your feet but, hey, Ms. SAS, you know your comfort level! Hosiery is only necessary if you need the completed look to help you imagine if you like or do not like an outfit. Wear makeup to achieve a clear picture of how a color enhances you.

Take water and snacks in the car. You may need them to sustain yourself as the day grows long. Preparation is nine-tenths of success. Dehydration causes fatigue. Rest as needed. Stop altogether if it isn't an 'up' day. Make sure you know the location of store restrooms.

Expect surprises! On most excursions, imagine a delightful Easter egg hunt. There will be some days, though, when you will walk away with nothing because you knew—and stuck to—your criteria:

1. Exceptional fit!
2. Only reasonable repairs you agree to do or hire.
3. The garment meets your wardrobe needs.

To feel great satisfaction, accept into your wardrobe only what you value. Unless you must have a new red dress—yesterday—be willing to wait for the best deals.

If you have a friend who cares for you and you believe her opinions add value—consider asking her to share a shopping day with you. Another fun outing occurs when several friends convene for the adventure. If the day produces few clothing results, you will have been refreshed with the valued friend factor. A friend is wonderful benefit these days.

When shopping, you might spot other attractive items not on your list. Yet the piece calls to you as a possible future need; e.g. a brand new turtleneck you will wear when yours becomes frayed or a newer ball cap that you remember your nephew wanted. This advice applies mostly to the lower cost thrift prices though you may buy for friends at consignment stores, also. Wash thrift purchases. With consignments, use your judgment.

In thrift stores, you may stumble upon a neat Halloween outfit. If your cash screams, like your toddler suffering a temper tantrum, to jump from your wallet for the 'deal', think first. Remember, Ms. SAS, you must serve yourself foremost by spending consciously. Now is also the time to experiment with unusual-for-you items that, when tried on, open a whole new vista. It is a perfect time to learn how you feel wearing something different.

One good reason to allow your cash to reign is for the special, benevolent reason of not passing up quality items that can be saved and provided as holiday, birthday and other gifts for the needy.

Chapter 4—Efficiency Scanning List

"He who buys what he does not need steals from himself."

Author Unknown

Efficiency transfers your finite time allotment to other fulfilling choices and fosters buying only what you need. As noted before, too many clothes create clutter and decision making delays. You must limit your excitement about the great deal until you carefully check the following points. A lot of items are in perfect shape, but others were donated for good reason. You will regret a $5 or $25 purchase when there was no way to repair the fault.

Quality fabric becomes the first component to search for after choosing the shopping aisle to begin the adventure. Always buy the highest quality items you can locate because they endure and look better, longer. Look for tightly woven fabric fibers and close stitching. To learn this, locate name brand tags on garments and look at the stitch length on the name brand. Compare several to see how loose and close stitches differ. Look for quality with an absence of tired, worn threads. Second, feel the fabric to verify its worth. You will learn with time and reading labels the difference between a quality cotton or wool and thin cotton or synthetics. See the check list below for more information.

If you choose to start with the skirts' aisle, visually seek smooth, sturdy fabrics to eliminate the need to touch every garment. Your goal will be to have learned enough from this book—and your own successes—that you do not put your hand on each item on the rack—wasting time. You will also rule out colors that do not compliment—saving you time. Grab items that draw your attention and, either then or at the dressing room, scan these criteria. These steps will become second nature for you:

1.   ***SHEEN:*** Look for 'shininess' which often means the fabric has been dry-cleaned and/or pressed with too hot an iron –this often appears near collars and cuffs and seams. It is a common problem with wool gabardine.

2.   ***FABRIC CONDITION:*** Feel and look for thinness, which is often an indicator of lesser quality fabric from the start or it can mean the weary garment saw its last days months ago. Regarding quality fabric I recommend natural fabrics: wool, cotton, silk, and linen, though the latter is better blended with other fabrics to decrease its wrinkles. Many synthetics do not 'breathe' so you will tend to sweat. They also cling and hold static electricity that might provide you with a new hair style. Quality rayon has a softer feel than cotton and drapes as nicely as many cottons. Refer to this site for a deeper review of the subject. http://home.howstuffworks.com/how-to-clean-natural-fabrics.htm

3.   ***SIZE:*** Pay attention when a stated size 'medium' really looks like a 'small' or 'large'. If cleaning instructions were not followed by the previous owner, the item may have shrunk and lost its resiliency; e.g. wool becomes smaller with a matted look, like a dog's fur that needed a brush

some weeks ago. Petites will measure shorter in the torso, sleeves and overall length which can work for slim, tall women if the item is a skirt, whose length does not matter. Some sleeveless tops can also pass your 'fit' test.   Watch for snug armholes that wouldn't be comfortable or attractive.

4.   ***IRREGULARS:*** Manufacturers sell defective garments. The item may look crisp and new at the store, but further scrutiny may reveal seams that lay across the chest in an unflattering way. Or, perhaps a huge print on the garment shouts to look at it, and not at you! Clothing you will most often reach for in your closet should beautifully compliment you.

5.   ***CARE & CLEANING:*** Look for the cleaning instructions near or under the name brand, or along the lower part of one of the seams. Decide if 'hand-washing' or 'dry clean only' is acceptable to you. Some items will not need dry cleaning, but wool certainly will, to avoid shortening its life by shrinking and matting it. Silk usually needs dry-cleaning, though some of lesser quality can be hand washed and ironed.

6. ***SEAMS & STITCHING:*** Look at seams for missing stitches. Can they be repaired by you or your seamstress? How close is the seam stitching? This will tell you the quality of the garment and the likelihood of its stitches coming undone without further securing the seams. If you pull each side of the seam apart you should not see light between it. Loose threads, appearing along the armhole seam of an exposed sleeveless top, look tacky.

7. ***PILLING:*** Look for pilling on fabrics, which looks like tiny round pills and signifies old, worn fabric. This happens when the garment contains synthetic fibers such as polyester, nylon, rayon and acrylics. Watch for exposed spandex threads on stretch wool garments.

8. ***POCKETS:*** Note if front pockets lie flat against the fabric or sag somewhat, which will detract from the presentation of even the finest fit. Location of the pockets is crucial. It is a rare woman who will look fashionable with large pockets at her hips. Seek slimming pockets that lie within the seam of a jacket or slacks. Pockets close to the breast line are acceptable, unless you are richly endowed, in which case be prepared to accentuate this body part. Be sure there are no

holes anywhere in or on the pockets; if there are, decide if you can or will reinforce them, by hand or machine.

9.   ***WHAT'S MISSING?*** Look for missing buttons or trim. Trim can be challenging to remove or replace; this would need to be asked of your seamstress. Sometimes an extra button is sewn in the seam. If not, and you love it, are you willing to purchase new replacements at a fabric store and trade out the old? You might find a similar button to match the missing one. An estimate for one inch replacement buttons is $1.50-$3.00 each.

10.   ***TINY HOLES and TEARS:*** Wool, especially cashmere, will often have minute holes from snacking moths; tears will occur on thinning fabrics or on a fragile fabric that collided with a doorknob or sharp object. Check carefully and hold the fabric up to a light to expose small holes. At the same time, watch for the next two points.

11.   ***PULLED THREADS/SNAGS:*** On sweaters and wool scarves, search for pulled or loose yarns. If small, they can be secured inside the sweater with similar colored plain thread, or

yarn, to stop any more snagging. Some jackets, such as 'boucle', feature yarns that are looped outward at intervals. Its fibers may start to look ragged rather than fashionable.

12. **ELBOW AREA:** Check here on thin fabric items and sweaters. Is it worn or threadbare from too many elbow encounters with the table?

13. **STAINS:** Check for stains and discolorations. If they appear discreet and/or on the surface, you can take a chance on home cleaning, or dry cleaning. Try a 'green' stain remover since they are usually less offending to fabric and thus much less apt to ruin it. Thrift stores generally have a return policy within a week to ten days. If you have the time and propensity, return the item if the stain remains. Ask about the return policy before purchasing and be prepared to swallow the cost in the unlikely event that your cleaning ruins the item. Consignment stores may also agree to your goal to try to free the stain. Again ask, as they generally have a no-return policy. However their chance for any sale if others also resist purchasing it are slim. Look for yellowing under the arm holes. Search for greasy stains embedded into the lap area of slacks, skirts or dresses. They're hard to remove.

14. ***BUTTONS, FASTENERS:*** Are all buttons present and secure? Can you hook fasteners such as on the skirt around your waist? Large buttons draw attention so avoid them on the backside. Unless you want to draw attention to your rear-end, yeah right! If the buttons on a blouse or jacket do not easily reach across to the buttonholes on the other side, the garment is too small. This applies to puckering when buttoned, which detracts. I recently bought a Banana Republic suit with two damaged buttons for $3.50. I bought replacement buttons for $10.50. I thrill at this classy $14 outfit!

15. ***ZIPPERS:*** Zip zippers several times to see if they are damaged in any way and make sure they 'catch' at the top so they do not slide down. If the zipper is the only problem—and price is right—and you do not want to let it go, your seamstress can likely replace it for a $12-20 charge. It will depend on the challenge of the fabric; velvet is a bear to work!

16. ***ELASTIC:*** Worn elastic will lack a strong snapping back effect as you stretch it, thus the garment has been washed too many times. New elastic could be substituted if the fabric does not

look worn or tired and its elastic 'floats' loosely within the casing.

17.   **VELCRO:** Check that Velcro still holds firmly. It can wear out and lose its 'stickiness'. Dependent on where it fastens to the garment, it can be replaced. Velcro comes in black or white or tan so be sure it will not be evident on a hot pink fabric.

18.   **LENGTHS:** Check that the following lengths are appropriate for you. Sit down to see how far the pant leg and skirt rise:

- a. Slacks, shorts, skirts.
- b. Dresses, and coat lengths.
- c. Sweaters, blouses, tops.
- d. Jacket sleeves and torso length.

Long sleeves need to end about ½ inch below the crack between the wrist and hand. Also note where it ends when the arm is bent to see if you accept that location.   If the length is too long, it can easily be hemmed up. If too short, avoid it since you cannot remove the cuff on a pant or sleeve without a line showing where the iron had pressed it flat many times.

Torso length is important to avoid accentuating the least attractive area at the hips.

19. **LININGS:** Many items need a lining, which is an exact sized replica of the main fabric. Jackets look so much richer with linings, usually made of thinner synthetic fabrics; e.g. acetate or polyester. Without a lining, wool pants will scratch and irritate or you will notice the wool fabric fibers sagging, such as at the rear-end. This garment looks sloppy versus draping well on your body. See-through summer cotton skirts often look better with a lining, however a slip will suffice. If a skirt is slim or the pants style simple, a lining could be inserted easily by a seamstress if you deem it worth the cost. Another option is to wear a "pant" slip.

20. **ADDED COSTS:** Don't forget to account for any added costs that you project will be needed to enliven the item, i.e. any dry-cleaning and tailoring. Again, avoid sewing or hemming velvet unless you wish a trip to your therapist.

21. **COLOR & MATCHING:** Besides looking vibrant in your best colors, consider another factor when mixing and matching. Lighter shades of a color will enhance a finished look if they are the

exact color base; i.e. aqua blue can be made of any number of combinations of blue and green. If the blends are slightly off they will detract. Do you have something to match this? Aim for no more than three colors when putting separates together, unless for example, the blouse has several colors in it from which you draw the two other colors for that outfit. A royal blue jacket and a rose pink blouse will be limited as far as matches unless you have the exact colors in a skirt or slacks, or a print that blends. White will work, however, the outfit needs a belt to tie them together. Ask yourself if you have a chain belt or colored one with those colors at home? Black might seem to work, however the brightness of the pink and the depth of the blue are not enhanced by the darkness of the black. Black in a print always pairs with solid black in the other items in the ensemble: blouse, skirt or slacks. Be mindful of the challenge of some matches.

22.   ***SHOULDER FIT:*** To avoid swimming in a top, make sure the shoulder seam line sits about 1/2 inch toward the neck, from the shoulder drop-off point. If it falls below the shoulder, it is the wrong size. This is not valid for garments designed to have dropped shoulders with seams about 2-3 inches below the shoulder line.

23.   ***FIT and COMFORT:*** If ever two words should wed, they are these. All the above factors have passed your tests, except the incessant itching the longer you stand gazing at the lovely garment. Another 'comfort' concern occurs if you suspect you will repeatedly be checking that the apparel stays in place versus regular adjusting; e.g. a nylon dress approaching your upper thigh. These irritants will drain you emotionally and relegate this otherwise perfect 'find' to the back of the closet. Not worth it!

24.   ***PETITES:*** If you are under 5'4" you will look your best in clothing made with your proportions in mind. Lighter colors on the lower half of your body enhance the overall look. See point #3 above.

25.   ***PROPORTION:*** Look in the full length mirror to see how these proportions do or do not enhance. Where does the hem rest on your leg? Where does the sleeve stop on your arm? The waistline needs to match your waistline unless the cut was fashioned to lie elsewhere.

Gather your prospective treasures. Try each on to see if it looks dowdy or outside your age bracket. Decide if it can be taken up easily. Does anything on the apparel cause it to stand out in body locations that you prefer not to announce? Does it cling? Does it hang, or drape well? Does the color enhance your features? Does the fabric's cut, meaning pattern cut, detract from an exceptional look for you? If you have pronounced curves, you will want to enhance them. Buy skirts or slacks with darts versus those featuring a boxy look. If you insist on a boxy jacket, make sure it is short and sports a flared skirt or slacks versus a pencil thin skirt or straight jeans/slacks cut. If the price tag is missing, the cost will often be priced at checkout—similarly to the lowest priced item in that category; e.g. dresses and vests.

Before leaving any thrift or consignment store assure you have not missed any bargain with your name on it. For consignment stores, ask the owner if there is anything new that you do not want to miss. She might not have priced them yet but she may allow you to look. In the thrift stores, check the restocking racks in the main aisles. Check the dressing room discards area.

After purchasing your treasures, complete the day by dropping off your articles that need dry-cleaning and placing others in the laundry basket.

Chapter 5—Wardrobe Maximization

"Nothing is a waste of time if you use the experience wisely."

Rodin

Much of the confusion behind the statement "I don't have a thing to wear!" lies in a sense of being overwhelmed. Your recently bought classy blouse is snuggled beside a velour pant and jacket outfit, plus you have not yet determined what will match that blouse anyway. Little wonder you cannot locate the skirt or slacks with which to mate it; there is no system to allow you to clearly see coordinating options.

Besides the seemingly missing wardrobe pieces, we overload the closet with even more purchases in an attempt to rectify the sense of lack. In the quest to resolve this supposed 'scarcity' of clothes, we end up with too many—and too disjointed. HINT: This habit, my fellow "frugality" experts, is the reason you are able to snap up bargains—available from others' discards.

The motto worth consideration: "Less is often more—when well chosen from the start!"

To that end, let's explore a fun, wardrobe organizing session I offer to Denver clients. The main goals are ease of dressing, elimination of complexity and the enjoyment of what you wear.

Plan a morning or afternoon time slot of 4-6 hours. Make sure there is natural daylight to see colors optimally. Make a serious attempt to locate and ask a trusted friend—who can appreciate your sense of style and whose sense of style you like—to join you in this closet and wardrobe renovation. Provide her tea, snacks, lunch, her favorite music, a cardboard statue of Brad Pitt, and any other comforts as gratitude for her gift to you. Champagne will really get your session going smoothly! Enjoy your excitement because this is a day that will provide so much simplicity to your life! BONUS: You will find these shared activities very delightful, special, and productive—so make them truly enjoyable. If you cannot recruit a helper, go ahead with treating yourself to good music and whatever else will please and motivate you.

For best use of time prepare the bedroom space ahead:

1. Place 3-6 clothing items that you most value to one side of the closet so you see your style and color favorites; i.e. what do you love to convey so you can wear more of this style and color?

2. Decide which closet and which season of clothes has priority for this sorting day.

3. Clear all the clothes and shoes from the closet if possible. Use the bed, living room and floor if necessary. If you cannot maneuver at all with everything removed from the closet, take out at least one half to allow for neatly replacing the true treasures as you proceed.

4. Arrange all the sweaters where you can see them. Place them on the 'cleaned'

closet floor. Or, you may place them on the shelves until you make assessments.

5. For sorting to eliminate excess, provide large trash bags or boxes.

6. These bags and boxes will allow you organization when transferred to:

    a. Thrift stores—if you do not wish to take your discards there, please call for pick-ups which some stores offer. Recycling is good for others and the earth.

    b. Consignment stores—for possible resale; if you know you do not intend to take clothes there, put them in the thrift store box.

    c. Friends—as gifts.

    d. Trash—if fabric is worn out. You might toss what you don't like or looks weary before your friend arrives.

    e. Cobbler for shoe repair—if you are unwilling to go to this effort, these shoes would become donations.

    f. Tailor or your sewing area—for clothes that need altering or repair. These would become donations if you know you will not visit the tailor.

7. Move extra hangers to the farthest side or out of the closet and nearby for later purchases. Limit extra hangers—and future purchases—to no more than 20 unless you plan to discard most of your wardrobe. HINT: less is best as you maintain a wardrobe you use and use often.

8. Consider colored plastic hangers, plus specific skirt hangers and slack hangers for this streamlined closet. Thrift stores offer these.

9. Provide the best lighting you can, preferably natural light nearby, since it shows colors best, and any stains or discolorations. Natural light allows for optimum mixing and matching. Bring in lamps to boost the lighting if needed.

10. Obtain a full length mirror.

11. Have ready access to accessories to experiment.

12. Before your friend arrives, vacuum the closet floor and shelves. A fresh start for your new space! See your therapist if these orders seem overwhelming!

13. Have plenty of water and light snacks nearby. You will be thirsty!

14. Place a blank notebook nearby for your friend to list needs to add to your wardrobe.

15. Be mindful of the chief goal to eliminate clothes that no longer call out, "Wear me!"

If you have extra time during this pre-organization, go through your lingerie to organize it and toss what needed tossing a year, or two ago. List any purchases you know you will need to make in the notebook you prepared. If time allows, sort hosiery and socks.

When your friend arrives, show her your pre-chosen three to six favorites so she captures what you most prefer and enjoy. Consider what shades of neutral colors suit you best. Cool neutrals include black, beige, white, grey, brown and navy with much black in it. Warm neutrals include navy with less black in the fibers. Also, warm neutrals include cream, which looks yellowish beige, camel, rust, gold and lighter browns. Consider which actual colors work best for your skin tones. Warm colors include: yellows, peach, coral, orange, any orange-reds, chartreuse, olive, lime green, aqua, and turquoise. Cool colors include: most whites, taupes, which is a beige-grey, black, grays, silver, purples, pure red, cranberry red, burgundy or wine reds, pinks, deep forest green, and teal blue-green. When the item is a print that has more than one color from the warm and cool families, does it appear to you overall to be cooler or warmer, as far as color? Place the garment within the section where the most predominant color will reside.

Preliminary questions to answer with your friend:

1.   What styles do you prefer to highlight most often? We return to how you spend the bulk of your days in a month! Casual, sexy, playful, sophisticated, classic, sporty?   If you are clueless of what style you want to project, ask, "Whose style do I admire?" KEY: Remove most, if not all, of clothing with a look you no longer

like; e.g. resign the classic style clothes to allow for the more chic look you have come to value! Accept that you want more of the comfort of knits, if you do!

2. Focus on 2-3 neutrals and 3-4 colors you like that also compliment your skin tone and hair color. KEY: Are the number of colors and neutrals balanced, i.e., not too many colors with few neutrals to coordinate and not too many neutrals lacking spice? Aim for the use of no more than three prominent colors in each full outfit; i.e. skirt, blouse, and jacket. You can have a print item with several colors within it; use three of those colors in the rest of your look, including shoes.

3. What do you love about this garment? Does it match many other items, making it a financial win since each pairing stretches your initial purchase price? Perhaps one blouse brings back memories you want to keep. Trust me; you can access the memory anytime without needing to save the clothing item. It is okay to have some items you are unsure of, but they go in a separate part of the

closet to re-evaluate during the next 1-3 weeks. When you feel how nice it is to wear what you love, you will find it easy to part with the items you question. KEY: "Do I reach for this piece often, and why or why not?"

4. What value will eight pairs of jeans provide you? Or eight suits when you no longer wear them? Or too many vests? Or handbags? At what point do too many items squander your energy, making dressing decisions that could better be used more creatively? KEY: Numbers of items will not provide fulfillment like quality, comfort and fit in every piece!

If your friend will assist, the time will pass quickly if she re-hangs the clothes as you remove them, placing them in the order noted in Chapter 6. She also will list your needs in the notebook as they become apparent.

Begin by trying on dresses as they are a stand-alone item—other than adding a jacket or nice sweater layered over it. Remember to work with only one season of clothes that day. I live in Colorado so I remove summer clothes in October, and return them in April or May, to effectively use the closet and drawer space for either season. When fabrics can overlap seasons, use them to the uttermost.

For each item, have your 'helper' ask what you feel about it: "Why do you love this?" Don't be surprised that you might suddenly wonder why you ever thought you liked it! Keep what delights you, versus staring into the closet wondering what you like enough to wear. HINT: Besides fitting well, you declare an end to allowing any item that does not reflect who you are to hang in your closet—wasting space. Although not mandatory, if you are over 50, you will find it in your best interest to delete wardrobe items that better suit a 25-40 year old. The secret to designing a wardrobe you are pleased with is adding clothing that enhances your essence and your proportions—not a model's, whether your age or younger.

Ask some deeper questions when you hesitate in answering what you like about it. "Do I wear this only because I do not wish to offend the giver?" If you need a ready excuse, should you be confronted by that giver, try this true response said with the joy and satisfaction within it: "I purged my closet of any and all clothes that I do not totally love to wear."

A last question entails facing your financial mistakes head-on, and letting them go to expedite enjoying what you now know. Nothing is gained, but sorrow, if you insist on paying emotional debt to what you did not know previously. KEY: How many times in life do we not know until we do know? Get on with the business of efficient, joy-FUL living.

Have your friend tell you how she sees each piece enhancing your body type and the style you wish to portray. She can tell you if it looks 'tired' and on its last legs. I have worn outfits more than 40 times and they retained their quality look while others no more than ten times before they looked sloppy, e.g. synthetic fabric knit tops. Since 'sloppy' is not what I wish to portray, they go. Determine, in as natural a light as possible, if the color flatters your face or makes you look washed out. How comfortable does it feel sitting and reaching? Does anything about it bother you, and if so, do you like it enough to endure it?

If it passes these tests, look through the other options for matches you have not seen in tops or bottoms. Hold the item up to the light to see if the fabric textures harmonize and the colors coordinate. Try on the possible matches with the right shoes to see how the proportion looks. A classy look depends on proportion. Can you mate a soft draping top or jacket with a straight or slightly flared skirt to avoid looking boxy? Do you have nicely draped slacks to compliment a boxy jacket or sweater? Notice where the skirt length crosses your leg. A length just above the knee or higher enhances petites, unless any extra weight draws attention to that excess. Just below the knee or mid-calf honors taller or heavier women. Notice how attractive various spots on the leg look.

Your friend can write in the notebook what extras you need to buy to maximize outfits; i.e. seek to have three tops/blouses and three slacks/skirts, or dresses for each jacket. Look for belts and other accessories to finish the outfit. List all that is needed. You can purchase accessories often at retail clearance sales and consignment stores. You may find it more challenging to find belts and nice jewelry at thrift stores.

Try different ways to accessorize. What belt could accentuate the waist or hips, if it is long enough? Lower the neckline of any soft turtleneck sweaters by using a nice pin or brooch. Be aware of how the lowered neckline accentuates you or not. What dress or blouse displays exquisite fabric but does not draw you to it? Can you add a colorful scarf with a necklace on top of the scarf? Regarding scarves, they will stand out most when the print on the solid background is lighter than the darker background. Sheer scarves in silk drape better than synthetics.

Career dressing can mean so much more than suits lacking a feminine allure. Very nice sweaters can replace a jacket to compliment a skirt or dress. Bright colors in suits or jackets are acceptable. Bright skirts with a neutral jacket and vice versa might shine for you.

Casual clothes can look fabulous with a little intention. Add belts, scarves, or jewelry to draw attention to your quality long-sleeved T-shirt or plain sweater. Contrast bright colors against each other.

As you continue the process you will discover many unsuitable items. You will not benefit by dwelling on the hundreds of dollars you might have saved had you been aware of what would best suit you. Now you do know, so keeping a costly item with the wrong proportions or color will leave you irritated.

Chapter 6—Closet Organization

"Make all you can, save all you can, give all you can."

John Wesley

Create an efficient closet by hanging clothes according to this system: left to right or right to left. Dependent on the type of closet and how far you need to reach back beyond the edge of the door to obtain some items, you may like this color system to organize clothes: whites, off-whites, beiges, taupe, yellows, greens, blues, purples, reds, pinks, rust or orange, browns, grays, and blacks. Place the least used at a further distance, even another closet if space is challenging; e.g. evening clothes, opposite season clothing. If you must reach far back along the sides of the closet to retrieve items, place the neutrals in the middle with colors on either side.

The next recommendation demonstrates another system for hanging clothes. Organize each type of clothing within same color systems, e.g. casual T-shirts, if you prefer to hang them, short to long sleeved, within the white section. Some sweaters can hang without losing their shape though most need to be folded and shelved or in drawers. White blouses, white jackets, skirts, slacks and dresses hang in the white section.

Proceed to beiges as noted in the first paragraph. The advantage of this method is that you will be able to choose between several styles and fabrics among the 'beiges' or 'blacks' since they hang in one section.

My entire closet wardrobe, not including overcoats in a closet near the garage, uses nine feet of rod space. This includes two belt hangers, one handbag hanger, two shoe hangars, and both summer and winter clothing. If possible keep the other season clothing in another room.

Whichever system you choose, hang velour pantsuits and jeans on slack hangars on one end of the color spectrum and place evening clothes on the other end. As you see new connections for ensembles, hang them together initially—to remind you of what you created. Seeing a scarf draped on a blouse will remind you to accessorize with it.

Dependent on the available shelf or drawer space, organize sweaters and jersey tops and turtlenecks, also by color, if possible. T-shirts that are not hung need to be sorted in one place, as are socks, hosiery and lingerie.

Handbags are arranged in a hanging bag or they can be stacked on a shelf. Ask yourself if you are willing to take time to change handbags to match specific clothing. If you are unwilling, remove those you know you will not use. If you do choose to keep some or all, assess that they blend with the prominent colors you wear. Fashion requests bright bags at times to accentuate the outfit. Yet, when this occurs, remember that cool colors will stand out best with cool colors, and warm with warm. See Chapter 1, mid to latter portion, for a 'colors' refresher.

Shoes can also be hung in shoe bags or placed by color on the floor, on shoe racks, or on shelves. Now is the time to look closely at the condition of those shoes and boots. Sloppy shoes do not feature your great garments very well. Regarding winter gloves and scarves, keep them near coats, which are by the door.

Realize that this experience will grant you big rewards. Give yourself the satisfaction of eliminating unneeded items! When finished with the sorting day, move the assigned thrift, consignment and tailoring boxes or bags to the proper destinations as soon as possible.

The goal remains: be as streamlined as possible, keeping that which delights and works for you. To maintain order, you need to commit to keeping this organization that saves time and energy. You will know what is missing to be able to add it. Mark in your reminder device or on a calendar a date in 4-6 months to re-organize.

You may maintain this system—to benefit you—by exerting the least energy on clothing choices. Purge and organize twice yearly when the seasons change. Discard an item as you welcome a new purchase.

At the end of this productive day, you opened the space for the wardrobe pieces you will soon locate—as you wait for them to surface.

After the effort you put forth and the result you accomplished, make the time to enjoy a long gaze at your closet when finished, and again each successive morning. You created efficiency and beauty, and found it fun.

Rejoice at the skills you added to your repertoire to better use in the future!

Chapter 7—Conservation Equals Your Abundance

"By sowing frugality we reap liberty, a golden harvest."

Agesilaus

So what abundance could there be in conserving and frugality? You seldom hear the word 'frugality' in conversation in the last few decades. It may sound at first foolish, valueless, and certainly old fashioned.

Frugality, as defined by Wikipedia entails the practice of:

1.   Acquiring goods and services in a restrained manner.

2.   Resourcefully using already owned economic goods and services to achieve long term goals.

If frugality and thrifty shopping suggest limitation to you, who would want or welcome that, you wonder? If your mind races ahead to equate conservation with denial of pleasure in buying new apparel—please suspend that impression.

Instead of denial or miserliness, think expansion. Will you agree to look with fresh eyes and senses attuned to what fulfillment means for you? Reinforce this idea: your unique choice of spending money, based on your values, will provide showers of abundance.

Can you honestly say that the numerous consuming…err…shopping outings you have taken have brought you as much peaceful or sensual fulfillment as a leisurely walk, or restful breathing, or a run in beautiful surroundings? Ponder that! Mentally revisit your last nature walk when you viewed a sunset or rainbow. Recall how non-material it seemed—yet, oh so nurturing.

Ask yourself if enriching times spent with someone you like and love—even cleaning the house—in any way matches the satisfaction of accumulating ever more things?

This chapter returns us to the issue of values. Given one earthly life, how would you want to have it spent for the best return on your investment? ***Your Money or Your Life*** by Vicki Allen and Joe Dominguez highlights life qualities. The new revised version adds Monique Tilford as an author. One of the hallmarks of this book teaches the correlation of trading one's life energy, consumed in hours spent earning money, for whatever value you embrace. The authors demonstrate how a frivolous waste of life energy on anything but what satisfies, lacks logic.

Spend some time doing Allen's book exercises. Become aware and clear of what will fulfill you overall. From that vantage point, focus your time and money on those options. Their website is noted with the online courses in Chapter 9.

When you are conscious of what you will trade your life energy for to have the life you most desire—the places you shop and how much you spend will matter.

The definition of frugality may seem somewhat foreign to Americans who have been accustomed to little restraint. If restraint seems a limiting concept, consider that you gave it its meaning by accepting the defining word: 'limiting'. What if restraint were to mean expansiveness toward what you cherish? Would not frugality then actually be a gift? Great news lies ahead so stay with me awhile!

Many Americans, unlike so much of the world, have had the luxury of endless raging consumer dissatisfactions that they self-medicated with credit cards, cash, addictions and other means. Advertising succeeded in baiting our appetites while our sense of entitlement kicked into gear. Add to this that consuming obsessions produce unhealthy stress.

One of the detriments of Americans' 'have it all' mentality has been resistance to anything that was not novel—and instantly gratifying. Most folks who endured the 1930's depression still exhibit frugal ways that are seen as old fashioned, and thus obsolete. After all, few middle and upper class Americans have lacked access to or appetite for, anything they fancied: cars, travel, a plethora of entertainment options, adult sports and other toys, technological gadgets touted to supposedly make life simpler, the latest styles and many extras unknown to previous generations. Tanning booths, massages, any number of beauty salon hair and skin treatments, personal trainers, life and business coaches all became a citizen birthright or at the least, options.

For many Americans there has been a subtle sense of entitlement for nearly all they could want. If we could earn it, we felt we deserved to treat ourselves to whatever presented on America's ample buffet. Leanness was not in the lexicon of most baby boomers and their children. There might be some juggling of priorities as far as which desire manifested first but credit cards could often solve that.

To regain a sense of fulfillment you might have lost along the way, take time to contemplate how meaningful some of your various purchases have been. Design some quiet time to really look at choices asking, "How much pleasure does, or did this provide me?" This could include choices in any of these categories: groceries, computer, TV or music equipment, cars, sports equipment, trips and other experiences created to make memories. If looking at the purchased item or a picture of the event still thrills you, you will feel that same wonderful gratitude anew. For me, it occurs as a warm flush of feeling in my chest.

Giving thanks for selected people, places and things fulfills us. The advantage of ***Your Money or Your Life*** lies in its training to learn to focus the greater share of finances where the most fulfillments lie. Many women who shop the way my book teaches gain the pleasure of spending more money on a commodity or experience other than more costly clothing, should they wish. A classic example of substitution of outlay of money can be found in gardening to supplement the grocery bill—with more soul benefits than financial.

You can imagine how conserving in one area yields abundance for the places your top values live. You still spend, which keeps the economy flowing, but where the money lands changes. Keeping your 'valued' choice in the front of your mind will require training since our thinking easily defaults to unawareness and previously learned automatic behaviors, especially a pesky sense of lack. Choose to be aware and congruent for the rich fulfillment it provides.

Despite how we humans tend to wallow in the victimhood of little or no choice in matters, we are always free to choose for ourselves, if only in the powerful choice of our response! If a purchase has lost its wonder, note this awareness and learn from it. Jot down the things, from the list of all you possess—or have experienced—that pleased you greatly, as well as what has not. People tend to become self-judgmental when their frivolous purchasing stares them in the face. Be assured, self-judgment produces nothing of worth for you.

In contrast, acute awareness energizes for forward movement. Besides, consider how often in the past you learned through various other life mistakes. Just move ahead to the next step in designing a life you want; don't linger in the past.

Anything that you come to discover as excessive for you, based on your values, robs your life of simplicity. This may have occurred with already spent thousands of dollars that could have brought you closer to financial freedom. Perhaps the clutter robs you of energy!

Here are a few fulfillment strategies to begin or reinstitute:

• Quality times with friends and family—cooking and eating together, hiking, singing, beautifying your community, reading aloud, playing board games or cards, and sharing any of the next listed items

• Creative pursuits such as writing, drawing, cooking, renovating furniture or the home environment, musical developments, gardening, jewelry design, pottery, and acting

• Life-giving times in nature or in the silence, perhaps meditating

• Volunteering—generosity goes a long way for your soul and the planet's sustainability

• Developing civic pursuits or a career in your area of passion

• True recreation—bicycling, bowling, hiking, skiing, dancing, volleyball, tennis, etc.

• Learning through reading, attending lectures such as in bookstores, renting documentaries and travel videos from the library, taking a class, enjoying a book club and its socialization

• Supporting theater productions, live comedy, sports events, art shows, etc.

• Savoring solo retreats to connect with yourself

To experiment with any of these strategies, ask yourself, "What would I add to the list to feel fulfilled, in place of an impulsive shopping spree?" Would you linger over the taste of your favorite dessert or cup of coffee with trusted friends in a beautiful setting? Would you play with people you like and love in some spontaneous way? Would you appreciate nourishing foods from your own garden or local vendors? For an extra surprising treat, share one tenth of that bounty with the community. Will you write poetry and share it at local coffee shops? Most poets excel at supporting each other's creative endeavors as do many other creative ventures.

If you do not know what frugal opportunity attracts you, begin with trying some different things regularly, preferably with little cost. Complete this book's experiment of organizing your closet or seek help to organize any other part of your home or garage. Design a conserving lifestyle—not a miserly one—as you accumulate only what you need to decrease clutter. Clutter absorbs physical spaces and the brain, when decisions must be made amongst many choices.

For a month, try this frugality experiment. Focus your daily life on appreciating the use of what you have and acquiring only what you need. This goal would mean miserliness if you defined it that way. Use a definition that focuses on simplicity and deep fulfillment as you trade emotional and social pleasures for stuff. To maintain focus keep a list near and convenient for you—perhaps at the kitchen table—to relish your deeper appreciations. This list goes hand in hand with the fulfillment of thankfulness, which will be presented in Chapter 10.

One of the joys of becoming a seriously aware shopper (SAS) will be a soul-refreshing return to simplicity. Whatever catapulted the U.S. to its current level of consumer ideology decreased the quality of life for many.

If tougher times and tighter financial resources impose decreased consumerism, these advantages will be valuable from a conservation minded perspective:

- The satisfaction of knowing this book's shopping strategy to maximize the wardrobe you choose rather than a haphazard collection

- More time with cherished friends and family as you spend less time trading hard earned money for careless entertainment

- More times enjoying one's own company

- Quality memories from sharing tasks that build community

May you bask in a values-driven abundant and conservative lifestyle!

Chapter 8—Other Nifty Thrifty Deals

"It is thrifty to prepare today for the wants of tomorrow."

Aesop

Thrift mindedness can expand into other avenues for pampering yourself. You might explore discounted massages, facials and pedicures from students at reputable schools.

You may enjoy such services despite limited funds. The instructors of those schools are nearby and you can request information from them. The drawback of this choice yields service from a 'tentative' student versus a confident practitioner. A professional knows the right pressure without being coached. With nail services, there may be rare times when the polishing is not perfect. You have the opportunity to practice requesting what you want—asking more than once if needed. Asserting our needs pertains to any other services, whether at the bank or shopping. We should expect 'service' wherever we take our business.

eBay offers a selling option if you wish, however there is a big learning curve for selling. You will need to read the eBay tutorial. Selling on eBay requires careful bookkeeping regarding who owes you money before you send the item.

If you become good at locating deals that may profit you on eBay, here are some components to learn:

- Deciding what is worth your time to offer for sale and a commitment to thoroughness as you seek to make money.

- Importance of revealing any flaws in the item, i.e., do not try to hide anything since as a seller you will be rated on your product, as well as your service. Ratings matter if you choose to continue to sell.

- Expert photography with at least three pictures, including angles—to demonstrate product condition.

- Well-written description of the item that will compel a purchase, noting any disclaimers for each item to cover yourself legally.

- Choice of mailing option, realizing this cost may be high so you must account for it in your price, and choice of your promised turn around time. The post office will pick up several items at your home if you sell a lot.

- Monitoring your auction during the bidding process; e.g. there will likely be questions you must allow time to answer.

- Choosing the length of time you will run your auction and a good ending point; e.g. weekend or evenings.

Coupons are available at thrift stores for upcoming sale days and as you bring in discarded items. Check also online at thrift stores for coupons, e.g. www.ARCThriftPromotions.com.

Custom clothing made by you or your seamstress will afford excellent fit, the finest fabric options, and the ability to add to your wardrobe a matched print blouse to complement skirts and slacks. Consider learning this sewing skill since it will re-emerge in the coming years. It can offer a creative, cost effective outlet if you have not tried it. If not a full-fledged effort, the skill will afford you the ability to do minor, or major revisions. We each decide where to spend our precious time. Is this a creative endeavor for you?

The web site, www.Craigslist.com, offers clothing for purchase. Find men's and women's boots, maternity clothing, children's clothing in bulk, sunglasses, wedding and evening gowns, and brand name handbags . You need to know the difference between an original and a knock-off, which is a fake of an original. It is best to see items before purchasing to save everyone's time and to verify that the value suffices.

Furniture consignment stores offer unusual creations with sturdy woods, leathers and plush fabrics. Many feature used model home items, essentially non-used. You still need to sit on the furniture to notice if it is sturdy and comfortable.

Chapter 9—Referrals for Conscious Consumption

"With greater emphasis on working to live, not living to work, we are creating awareness for simpler solutions, a more creative existence with healthier, happier longevity, for those brave enough to accept the challenge."

Tracey Smith

Consider these books:

Your Money or Your Life, Vicki Robin—very practical guide for use of money to reflect your values and yield resultant savings!
Tightwad Gazette, Amy Dacyczyn—hundreds of thrift tips.

Try these web sites:

www.simpleliving.net This web site offers many ideas to simplify your life. For online groups, you can study ***Your Money or Your Life***. Select 'online study groups' after entering this web site. These groups address financial integrity. You will pay a nominal fee for this invaluable guidance that will save you more than the program costs—while increasing fulfillment.

www.storyofstuff.com This 20 minute video presentation, good for you and your kids. It is fun while the reality shown will encourage you toward a new mindset.

Contrary to what the past decades have exhibited in America, the globe cannot sustain an endless consuming/wasting pattern without greater harm thrust upon our planet home.

www.freecycle.com This site offers places to give your things, and gain items for free.

www.bargainist.com This website claims to locate the best deals available. They offer coupons for items.

www.financialintegrity.org   More on living congruently!

www.populationmedia.org   Watch the ticker in the center of the page for the speed at which our world overloads itself!

www.transitionus.org   Grass roots movement: "Designed to achieve re-localization at the community level, currently representing one of the most promising ways of engaging people and communities in strengthening themselves against the effects of these monumental challenges— climate change and peak oil." The networking results in a life that is more fulfilling, socially connected and resilient.

www.thesuntribe.com/sustainableliving.htm A superb sustainability list to print and view often for actions to explore. You will enhance simplicity.

REFERRALS TO LOCATE THRIFT AND CONSIGNMENT STORES

Search www.google.com   website. Type 'thrift stores, name of your city' or the closest city name in the address section.   Example: Thrift stores

Atlanta, GA. If one of the early options is <u>www.citysearch.com</u> , this link will provide stores that include consignments for clothing and if available, for house wares. They are rated based on reviewers; however, trust your own assessment to be your best judgment.

Chapter 10—Celebration

*"How simple and frugal a thing is happiness:
a glass of wine, a roast chestnut, a wretched
little brazier, the sound of the sea. . . All that is
required to feel that here and now is happiness is a
simple, frugal heart."*

Nikos Kazantzakis

Planned and unplanned celebrations lack in this fast paced world. Celebration rituals enliven us. We too often rush to the next goal before savoring the sweetness of the "dessert of accomplishment."

Do you remember the valued reason for choosing to educate yourself about thrift shopping? By focusing on what you gained from it, your mind runs a computer search for the benefits. When you recount these, any sense of lack will dissipate and your life will feel bigger and better—at least for the moment.

However, former patterns of thinking might resurface, stealing the satisfaction of saved finances and quality purchases. Americans' omnipresent sense of lack can arise just as much while thrift shopping as from forgetting the thrill of full-priced purchases they have made.

Note the common denominator: thinking. Notice lack, and your life will constrict with a lingering 'not enough' feeling. Think thoughts of abundance and gratitude—throughout your daily life choices—and life flourishes. With this attitude, you can make every day celebratory.

One way to practice pleasurable feelings is to name a few valued parts of your life. Here are some suggestions. You may add your own:

- A full tummy
- Any degree of health you experience
- Absence of pain
- Physical senses that you enjoy: vision, hearing, smell, taste, touch
- Loved ones who enrich your life
- Vast opportunities in America
- Nature's supreme gifts—rain showers, lakes, mountains, sunlight, etc.

- A bath or shower
- Fresh water to drink, unlike at least a third of the world's population
- Spiritual and emotional expansion
- Abundant time for creativity
- Abundant opportunity to shape little lives, if a parent
- Warmth or coolness

HINT: Allow yourself to linger over the expansion of this list. Slow down to celebrate your enrichments. Yes, experiment with slowing down. Breathe slowly, daydream, and contemplate without making a list—preferably while in nature.

Another way to feel the goodness in your life would include listing the prices—and thus saved money—for the clothing treasures you found. If of value to you, note the purchase prices on your computer, or in a daily planner, or inside the closet door.

I note my deals because reviewing my clothing list of the last 24 years reminds me of the delight of perfect surprises—in my preferred price range.
I have saved thousands of dollars since I first began thrift shopping for my wardrobe purchases. I could have spent those thousands paying more for clothing. I chose to honor my higher values: recreation with loved ones and savings.

Saving money through conscious choices feels fabulous, doesn't it? Did you find hidden 'Easter eggs' in your clothing hunts?

Celebrate the big successes and the smallest of things. Feel grateful often. How rich and simple is that? May you ever enjoy the rewards of thrifty savings!

About The Author:

Sandi Lynn is a life coach and registered nurse dedicated to offering people life-enhancing options for wholeness: physically, mentally, financially and in relationships. Sandi enjoys connecting others to resources that expand them. She provides individual and group coaching toward maximizing each person's inherent wholeness. Other services are noted at her website: www.accesswholeness.com

Sandi celebrates life while enjoying creative cooking of healthy food, dancing, meditating, hiking, camping, canoeing, skiing and learning. She raised two sons with the information that created this book and counts as among her richest abundance those two great human beings. She lives a thrifty life with her wild and crazy mountain man husband in Golden, Colorado.

Cover shot taken in Ali's Closet in Centennial, Colorado, website:

www.sites.google.com/site/alisclosethr/

www.ingramcontent.com/pod-product-compliance
Lightning Source LLC
Chambersburg PA
CBHW031256280526
45784CB00004B/1873